American Football & Passover

A Playlet about Plagues

MATHEW R. SGAN

Library of Congress Control Number: 2021924551

HARDBACK: 978-1-956803-71-6 ($21.99)
PAPERBACK: 978-1-956803-70-9 ($13.99)
EBOOK: 978-1-956803-72-3 ($5.99)

Ordering Information:

For orders and inquiries, please contact:
1-888-404-1388
www.goldtouchpress.com
book.orders@goldtouchpress.com

Printed in the United States of America

Contents

About the Author

Author Mathew R. Sgan was born in Medford Massachusetts USA in 1934, He received a B.A. from The University of Massachusetts-Amherst in 1956; a M.A. from Colgate University in 1958; and a Ph.D. from Cornell University in 1963.

Sgan served was an academic advisor at the University of Minnesota in 1961-1962. He then spent 15 years at Brandeis University, where he served as Dean of Students and Dean of Admissions and Financial Aid. He followed that position with a stint as an academic Associate Dean at the University of Massachusetts-Dartmouth.

In subsequent years, he wrote a book titled *The Boston Book of Sports: From Puritans to Professionals.* As an outgrowth of the book's research, he co-founded the *Boston Museum of Sports.* That program is now housed in the T.D. Banknorth Garden in Boston Massachusetts.

While at Cornell, Sgan married Mabel 'Gin' Lum Sgan of Hawaii. She also received her Ph.D. degree from Cornell in 1963. In 2000, upon her retirement from college teaching, they moved to her birth site, Honolulu Hawaii. Mathew and Gin have two children and five grandchildren. Gin passed away of natural causes in 2015.

As Executive Vice President of the *Arizona Memorial Museum Association, Mathew* led the development team that eventually raised the public-private funds (some $54 million) necessary to replace the Visitor Center and Museum at the USS *Arizona* Memorial in Pearl Harbor. The replacement structure was dedicated in 2010.

Sgan is an active member of the Conservative Jewish Congregation, Sof Ma'arav, in Honolulu Hawaii. Sof Ma'arav means 'farthest west.'

It is taken from a poem by Yehuda Halevi, an 11th-12th century CE Jewish physician, philosopher, and poet.

Books by Mathew R Sgan

The Boston Book of Sports: *From Puritans to Professionals* 2008 Xlibris Publishing

Fried Matzah for Breakfast: *A Family Memoir* 2012 (with brother Dr. Arnold Don Sgan (z"l) and niece Karen Small (z"l)

Honey and Poi: The Origins and Development of Congregation Sof Ma'arav in Honolulu Hawai'i 2018 (with Dr. Alex Golub) Xlibris Publishing

Appendix Compiled in Conjunction with *Honey and Poi* 2018

Torah and Taro: Jewish Contributions to Hawaii 2020 Xlibris Publishing

Illustrator Hunter Hughes

Hunter Hughes lives and works in Honolulu Hawaii as an illustrator and creative professional. He studied animation at the University of Hawaii-Manoa where he also played football. Much like this playlet, bringing sports, art, and faith together is one of Hunter's passions. He also helps young athletes get better at sports through videos on Tik Tok and YouTube under a program called 'All Around Athlete.''. His presentations have been seen by millions and he helps to make a lasting positive developmental impact on young people through combining art, technology, and sports. Hunter is a tournament golfer and works as a pro trainer at golf clubs on Oahu.

Rituals: Leader's Determination

The Seder

Here are some suggestions for those groups that are including the playlet in place of a second night of Passover seder.

The table should be set for a conventional seder. A seder plate is placed before the leader. It contains: Bitter Herbs (could be horse-radish); hardboiled egg; Karpas (parsley or celery); Chazeret (Romaine lettuce); Roasted Shank bone and Charoset (mixture of chopped apples, nuts, cinnamon and wine.) The table also has bottles of wine; a dish or two for salt water; a large glass for Elijah, and a plate with three whole pieces of Matzah on it wrapped in cloth.

Certain ceremonies occur before the playgues take place. Say Kiddush and drink the first cup of wine. Washing of the hands is then done. Dip the karpas into the salt water and pass it around. Hold up the plate with three pieces of matzah and break the middle piece in two. Hide one half of the middle matzah. It is the afikomen. Children will search for it and the one who finds it usually receives an award.

Seder Plate

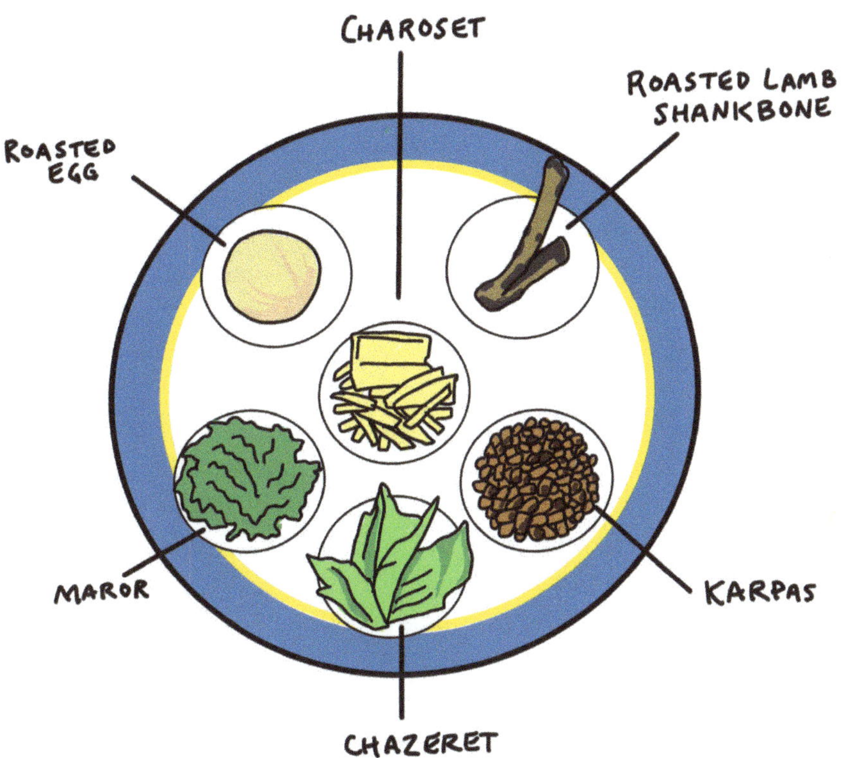

Pre-Game	During Game Script	Post-Game
Kiddush-First Cup of Wine	The Four Questions	Grace-Third Cup of Wine
Washing of Hands	The Four Sons	Hallel-Fourth Cup of Wine
Karpas	The Ten Plagues	Songs
Break Middle Matzah	Dayainu	
	Second Cup of Wine	
	Matzah Blessing	

Bitter Herbs
Korech: Maror and Charoses
= A Hillel Sandwich

The Playlet

In this playlet, narrative and illustrations are used to tell the story of the Israelite Exodus from Egypt some 3300 years ago as a battle between theological foundations and belief systems. Haggadim have told this story in many variations through the ages. Recent titles are *Sci-Fi Seder* and *Harry Potter and 10 Commands*. Young adults especially, it is hoped, will be interested in this different approach to the story of Passover and its meaning in current times and terms.

The material is presented in a picturesque and humorous way while at the same time intending. deeper meanings. Much depends on the leader's preparation, a willingness of seder attendees to participate fully, and their creativity. The playlet highlights this wonderful story with numerous football, biblical, historical, and artistic directions and references to maintain interest and learning.

American Football and Passover may supplement the seder traditions, rituals, and symbols or it may stand alone. The story of the Exodus is thus elaborated and extended to whet further interest on and study of Judaism, Jewishness, the Exodus, and Passover.

If the playlet is used as an addon or as a teaching booklet rather than a religious ceremony, the arrangements above may be tempered as the leaders determine what best suits their purpose. Attendees should be encouraged to raise questions about the script and offer comments, relevant thoughts, and extensions about Passover and American Football, The idea is to maintain interest, involvement, and learning. Sometimes obviously; sometimes subtly.

The Appendices

Appendices are added to encourage further fun, presentation, and study activity, including how to encourage interest and involvement in the readings and discussion points. A sort of teacher's guide of 10 study questions suggests ways that, without risking embarrassment, participants of all ages can speak up about various facets of the Passover story and thereby understand its implication and significance better. There are directions and assistance to leaders which recommend how to proceed. Once again, much depends on a good leader.

Acknowledgements and Dedication

This approach to presenting the Haggadah in a unique almost irreverent style has been brewing for many years. Perhaps it began at the table of a Ukrainian immigrant grandfather who read the Hebrew in response to the questions of the young children at the seder. He read on in the face of side discussions, matzah nibbling, and a noise level that shook the house that he and his family built on a small junk yard cum farm on an acre or so in Medford, Massachusetts.

For the author, Mathew Sgan, as a young boy, the seders were the high spot of the year for his Jewishness. There was in the beginning really no religious component to his life except this funny language and this unique experience unfolding at a big dining room table for a couple of nights during the year. Medford had no Jewish community at the time., Saturday was just the sixth day of work during the week and even the High Holidays-Rosh Hashanah and Yom Kippur-were largely unattended and unnoticed. Sukkot and Shuvuoth were not even acknowledged. There was always work to be done. Food production and animal care on the farm took first place during the depression years.

Yiddish was the language of choice in the house. The author's immigrant grandmother communicated solely in it. His father also spoke Yiddish and had a basic religious education in a cheder in Poland/Lithuania He too was busy trying to make a living as a house painter and his interests, beyond that responsibility, centered mostly on politics and theatre. For such interests, he was active at what then was called the Workmen's Circle. A secular Jewish socialist club.

Given that background, the author's Jewish association had some foundation. It grew stronger when he led seders for his family and clan. began to do what he could to maintain interest in the important holiday of Passover. He took it personally and spent considerable time in preparation for the seders. He wanted to insure that the next generations of Jews in his family would embrace and enhance their religious celebrations of Passover.

The stage which encouraged this playlet, *American Football and Passover*, arose as a result of the author's participation in study and research into historical Judaism. He is indebted especially to the members of Congregation Sof Ma'arav in Honolulu, Hawai'i who have tutored and shared insights, references, and values about all phases of Judaism with him. That sharing was valuable both in the knowledge it provided and the duty it shed on him to do something of value for extending Judaism and Jewishness to present and future generations of his people.

To the Passover Story of the Israelites
and non-Israelites
Who miraculously gained release from Egyptian slavery
and transformed themselves, their descendants,
and the World forever

The Cast

Cast of Characters in Order of Appearance, Roles, and Scene

Character	Role	Appearance
God	I am that I Am;	Forever, Hashem
Narrator	Story line & Stage Direction	Throughout
Huti	Booth Announcer	Pregame
Tuti	Booth Announcer	Pregame
Thuti	Field Announcer	Pregame
Ads	Sponsors	Pregame & Halftime
Amun	Playgue by Playgue Announcer	Game Time
Bayisru	Playgue Color Announcer	Game Time
Moses	Israelite Prophet	Throughout
Aaron	Israelite Priest	Throughout
Pharaoh	Egyptian King and god	Throughout
Hyksos	Officials	Throughout
Royals' Team	Egyptian Players	Throughout
Ragtag Team	Israelite Players	Throughout
Fans	Egyptians	Throughout
Fans	Israelites	Throughout
Cheerleaders	Egyptian	Throughout
Cheerleaders	Israelite	Throughout
Snake	Varied	Often
Blood-Frogs-Gnats	Playgues 1-3	First Quarter
Poti-phar	Egyptian Assistant Coach	Often
Poti-near	Egyptian Assistant Coach	Often

Potti-go	Egyptian Assistant Coach	Often
Insects-Murrain-Boils	Playgues 4-6	Second Quarter
Hail-Locusts-Darkness	Playgues 7-9	Third Quarter
Passover	Playgue 10	Fourth Quarter
Pliny the Elder	Press Interviews MC	Post Game
Senebkay	Reporter	Post Game
Woreribe	Reporter	Post Game
Beizel	Reporter	Post Game
Mandlin	Reporter	Post game
Miriam	Sister of Moses & Aaron	Post Game
Nachshon	Volunteer, Red Sea Zone	Overtime

The Principal Actors

God- Known by many names but mostly referred to as 'I Am That I am' or 'Hashem' (the name.) Seems to have neglected what was happening to his chosen people in Egypt. Finally, hearing the Israelites moans and groans, moved against those who were enslaving them. That move changed their fortune and all of civilization. His big plan included establishing world-wide notoriety and a new code for life's conduct. Recognized that transformation requires a new generation and provided for a delay in the return to the promised land. His decrees and commandments have been involved in the major events in Jewish and world history.

Moses-Interesting choice as a superhero (GOAT) although in hind sight a perfect pick for the Jewish franchise. Humble beginnings, noble upbringing, and mysterious reconnections with his people well prepared him for the stupendous and demanding task of facing up to the major world figure of the time. Moses took his job seriously. Willingly took notes and served as a scribe to Hashem. Moses was not reluctant to challenge worldly and other worldly forces to complete his assigned task. He managed to succeed, but some errors along the way cost him a victory march into the promised land.

Aaron- Big brother who held things together until younger brother Moses arrived to lead the team in playgue diplomacy. Aaron was suited up and on call from the very opening of Moses' return and helped with presentations to the Pharaoh and his staff.. Moses recognized Aaron's importance and gave him a significant role in the dramatic events that followed. Moses even overlooked a few major errors (one whopper) that Aaron committed. Aaron also never made it to the promised land, but he did have a big time funeral.

*Pharao*h- Tried hard but really couldn't figure out what was going on. Surrounded by less than suitable advisors, he found that even when his defenses worked, they seemed to just lead to another losing battle. Kept equivocating which seemed to be itself what Hashem intended to take place. Tue final game winning playgue really shook him. In the very end, Pharaoh went too far. He lost face and troops. That over extension opened up the path for northern enemies to grab the center stage.of world power

Miriam- In the loop from the very beginning, she lent a nice touch to her family's leadership of the Jewish people. After a major role as a savior and caretaker of kid brother Moses, Miriam laid low for some time. Then when the troops crossed over the sea of reeds and the Egyptian troops didn't make it, she highlighted the accomplishment with a song poem. She earned a cup at the Seder table in recognitio0n of her contributions to the success of the Exodus.

YOU'RE
GOING
DOWN!

American Football and Passover
A Playlet on the Plagues

Script Contents

Appendices

American Football and Passover

Pre-Game Sponsor Ads

Narrator:
Here are some Ad themes. *Use your imagination* to suggest how they could be presented and extended for maximum fun and pun.[12]

Idols:
Fertility god ads
The right statue will help restore lust-- Buy the god that's best for you.
It's not easy with three wives.
Will also help your harvest.

Copy Centers
featuring the best in: Scrolls, Papyrus, & Parchment; Goose Quills; and Gall Nut ink.

No Flood Insurance
If the Nile doesn't flood, your insurance covers you
***Donkeys, Oxen, & Camels* for sale or lease**
Our transports will perform with confidence on all surfaces especially sand
Four leg drive provides great off-road capability
Cargo carrying superstars. New and used--
Buy now and get two humps for the price of one.
Yoking Oxen and Donkeys is not advisable.

SCROLLS, PAPYRUS, AND PARCHMENT

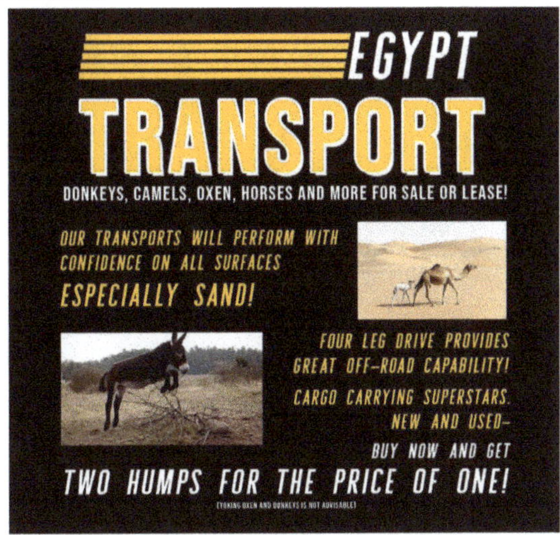

Act One

American Football and Passover:
A Playlet about Plagues

Narrator:	This is a play about the Hebrew Israelites leaving Egypt and attaining freedom from slavery as viewed through the prism of an American football contest. It is based on the Exodus story of Passover as found in the Torah and the Haggadah and the telling of that story at Seder commemorations of it. It features the Egyptian Royals versus *Israelite Rag tags*[1] for Divine Bragging Rights in that day. The Royals are the favorites and the spread is *nine*.[2] The Royals must survive all ten playgues to win. Over and under is *70*.[3]

We begin with two announcers with megaphones in a broadcasting 'booth.' In the background the ancient Egyptian populace moves about carrying sheaves of wheat, herding cattle, riding camels, and moving in chariots. Way back, city buildings are being built by slaves and there are Pyramids. A map of Egypt with various cities, the Nile, the Israelite Goshen area, and other areas is displayed behind the announcers.[4]

HUTI
TUTI

THUTI

Act I

Scene 1
In the Announcers Booth

Announcer HUTI: Welcome *polytheistic and monotheistic*[5] sports lovers. We have arrived at the moment of truth as to which super hero worship system is number one.

Announcer TUTI: Yes Huti-both of today's competitors of this is my God or your gods championship contest have earned their way to this epic contest.[6] The Egyptian Royals have won many world level battles including vanquishing the *Assyrians, the Persians, and the Babylonians*. The Israelite Rag tags have a less distinguished division based record, but they have managed to outplay the *Moab's, Midianites*, and other tribes to make it this far.[7]

HUTI: The Israelites will seek the answers to four questions during this game to explain why this game is different from all other games.

In all other games we can eat most snacks, but at this game only special snacks

In all other games, we can add many condiments, but at this game only special condiments.

In all other games, we do not mix bitter and sweet things but at this game we do it twice.

In all other games, we sit or stand, but at this game we relax and hope for a dramatic finish.

TUTI: Yes Huti those questions will be answered as well as how grateful the Israelites are to their coach and captains. We will also acknowledge four sons who suggest different ways (good and not so good) to understand these stories. There is a wise son, a wicked son, a simple son, and a distracted son who needs explanations and encouragement often. The idea is the more one understands the context of a game or event, the more one can improve oneself, help others, and contain their opponents.

HUTI: Right TUTI. We expect to see a formidable ground game by the Royals which the sons must be ready for. Word has it that the Israelites have developed a number of trick playgues as the basis of their game plan. They will have an aggressive defense against the Passover.

TUTi: Exactly HUTI. The Royals are expected to use a punishing ground game with fullback dives, handoffs, and a quick cut-out passing game. They will *offer lots of options.*[8] They will also intensify the work requirements of the Rag tags as the game progresses probably causing numerous injuries. No doubt there will be blood in the water!

HUTI:

On the Ragtag side, they will be leaning heavily on their *co-captain brothers, Moses and Aaron*[9,] who will be in touch with their playgue caller and following His playgue book. They hope to operate within a protected pocket. One advantage they will have is that they will receive their game plan wirelessly. Their playgues will be sent in from above. The Egyptian Royals will be tied to the old fashioned ways. They will have to signal formations and plays in the usual way. Those signals may be intercepted. With the field conditions promising to be much less than ideal, that might make a big difference.

Tuti:

Yes natural elements like wind flow, terrain, even animal and insect control promise to impact playgue-calling in this contest. Special teams and special effects will be very much in evidence in this contest,

HUTI:

Another Israelite Ragtag advantage is that *Captain Moses*[10] *was part of Royals team* until he was exiled on waivers for some alleged assaults on a Royals' worker. Of course, most of the witnesses have now passed on and *a lot has been forgotten.*[11]

Tuti:

A part of the Ragtag game plan is to be very patient. The word is that they will be taking it one playgue at a time. They are not looking for any quick outcome or breakaways. The Royals' plan is not well known, but if history prevails there will be stubborn resistance and lots of feints.

Act I

Scene 2
Down On the Field

TUTI: Welcome back. Thuti is down on the field with some news about the game plans of each of the teams.

Thuti: Thanks Goys. I just heard that the Ragtags will be using lots of *audibles and shotgun snaps*[13] as their game plan unfolds. That will be especially true if they get to the Red Sea zone. They will also overcome crowd noise by using a lot of hand and finger signals. Many of their playgues will be based on a spread attack and they will use an air raid offense often.

HUTI: What about the Royals?

Thuti: The Royals say that they will be stubborn[14] no matter what the field conditions are. They figure that the Ragtags have some tricky playgues up their tunics, but they are ready to cope with whatever comes up under their Pharaoh. They hope to create many pre snap illusions with players in motion, shifts and double shifts. The Royals expect a lot of quick release playgues.

TUTI: Anything more about the teams?

Thuti: Both the Royals and the Ragtags will rely heavily on their *staffs*. Both teams are relying on after contact and pass catch gains. Seems like they are depending on their staffs for decision making and for determining options. Staff positions are mostly filled although the Ragtag captains seem to have fewer key advisers at the game site and always are referring to help from above.

HUTI: Any name for that source of help?

Thuti: Very strange. They keep calling out – *I am that I am.*

HUTI: Right. Well we will see, what we will see. Thanks Thuti.

Narrator: **Pharaoh joins his principal advisors and they get in a motivational circle- rap inspiration led by Pharaoh-**

(Everyone)   No more straw and no more mortar
Lots more work and a bigger quota
They are just a bunch of shirkers

We will beat them into workers
On three, beat the monos'
1.2.3 beat the monos (Repeat)

Narrator: **Moses and Aaron get their team together in a motivational circle- They rap:**

(Everyone)   Our Lord has spoken and revealed his name
He indicated that we must play this game
He has heard our mourning about our defeats
And promises to deliver miraculous feats
One-two- three' Beat the Polys'
1-2-3 Beat the Polys   (Repeat)

Tuti: Well folks it looks like we are getting ready for the Rod Toss[15], so we will turn the mics over to playgue by playgue announcers *Amun and his partner Bayirsu* at the palace and along the Nile.

Act I

Scene 3
The Rod Toss and Opening Festivities

Amun: Thanks Huti, Tuti,and Thuti, now we are ready for the *Rod Toss*. Pharaoh and his principal advisors- Poti-far; Poti-near; and Poti-go are already standing by the Nile.

Bayirsu : And here come Aaron and Moses and their tribal band of Levite brothers. Moses promises to be a mobile, wildcat type quarterback with a lot of movement between *the river bank and the palace.* [16]Aaron will stick close to him to provide protection as well as offensive options as a wide out, fullback, or tail back. Their tight end is number achat-esray, Caleb.[17] He also scouts for them and knows the game.

Amun:	What a scene? Lutes, lyres, flutes, drums, strings, and cymbals. Music from both sides. The teams are taunting each other. Thuti can you tell what they are saying?
Thuti:	Oh the usual stuff. *We're number one. You shouldn't even be here. Go back to making mud and straw buildings. You're over hated.* It is getting quite heated though. The Israelites are chanting- we want more food and straw.
Bayirsu:	There is a *Hyksos officiating team[18]* and they are keeping the adversaries apart. Just in time too as the teams are bouncing up and down in place and something could break out soon. We've mic'd up Moses and Pharaoh for this exchange.
Moses:	Before the rod toss, I want to ask Pharaoh to let my people go. That is a request of the Lord, the God of Israelites.
Pharaoh:	Are you kidding? Nobody leaves until all the cities that I want are built. I don't even know that one whom you call the Lord. Get my servants back to work.
Amun:	The Israelites look dejected and they are grumbling about how tough things have become since Moses showed up. Moses and Aaron don't seem to be in great shape either. After all, Moses

is a free agent walk on. He was just a *shepherd[19]* when he was drafted. It is unclear what round it was. And Aaron may have been taken by surprise when Moses showed up in Goshen.

Bayirsu: But look. The people may have become weary but it appears that the chiefs of the various tribes are being reminded of their ancestry.[20] All the arranged marriages are making a difference as Moses and Aaron remind them just how many of them are related to one another and how they moved proudly troop team by troop team in history. Some of the records and their God speaking to their ancestors and making promises in those days, are being recalled. They are emboldening the Israelites.

Amun: Still Moses and Aaron are pretty old. They will be tested on all sides. The first test is up now. The Hyksos Referee told them to throw their rods down. Here comes the *Rod Toss*.[21]

Bayirsu: Wow, Aaron has thrown down his rod and it has turned into a serpent. But Pharaoh doesn't seem impressed. He is prodding his staff advisers and entourage into action.

Narrator: **Aaron's rod is brought to him by a cheerleader holding it as they do with the college flag at football games. A real show. Aaron takes the rod, twirls it over his head, and throws it down before Pharaoh.**

OH MY
RA!!!

The Royals rods are brought to them by chariot. The coaches and skilled players take the rods, throw them high in the air drum majorette style, and catch them. They then throw them down.

Amun: What a show! But wait, Pharaoh's magicians have tossed their rods down and they have become serpents. Now *Aaron's serpent* [22] *is swallowing* the magician's serpents. But Pharoah is not impressed. He keeps on saying and nodding 'no' to the Israelite request to go. He seems to be responding to some kind of outside influence.

Bayirsu: The Ragtags won the rod toss and will receive.

Amun: Some of the signs are great. My vote for the best Ragtag sign is: *Woe unto Pharaoh*! The Logo is a Burning Bush.

Bayirsu: Look at that Royals sign. *OuRA god is # 1.*[23] The Logo is a Snake on a Crown.

Amun: The Cheerleaders are lining the pathways from the Pyramids which are being used as team locker rooms to the field.

Bayirsu: How about the cheer leader outfits! The Royals are in Red & Gold form fitting Burquas.

Amun: And the Ragtags are in Blue and White Sadie Hawkins outfits.[24]

Narrator: Let's pause our playgues to look into the team locker rooms which are inside the Pyramids. Pharaoh is using a quill and a scroll and a papyrus blackboard on which he is marking defensive formations in hieroglyphics and looking for ways to stem the Israelite playgues.

The Royals' lockers are sarcophagus shaped.

In another room the Ragtags' lockers are ark shaped with pull cords and curtains.

Bayirsu: Here come the teams. The Royals have helmets; breastplates, and padded shoulders. Their numbers are in hieroglyphics.

Amun: The Ragtags have no padding and their numbers are in Hebrew. Number one is an aleph. The Ragtags chose to receive the kick off. The Royals have their backs to the Nile.

Act II

First Quarter Playgues: Blood, Frogs, Gnats

Narrator:	As we begin the contest Blood, Frogs, and Gnats- will be playgued out. The field of play is laid out with - *lean and fat cows* [25]are grazing among lean and fat corn.
	A boy in a multicolored coat is wandering around. The field is on the banks of the Nile.

The fans for both sides are seated on the pyramids -usual corporate like suites at top and more common bleachers at bottom. The Royals bench is throne like. The goal posts have snakes on the sides and the crossbar. Pharaoh is emerging from the Nile. He is confronted by Moses. Both men are mic'd up.

GO EGYPT!

Act II

Scene 1
Blood

Moses:	Look if we go through with this contest a lot of bad things are going to happen. Let my people go to worship our God on neutral ground. If not, I will strike the Nile with the rod toss winning rod and you will see blood in the water and throughout Egypt. We will launch blitzes into your trade lanes, storm the gaps, and clog up your game plans.
Pharaoh:	You will not succeed against our odd front defense. If I see blood in the Nile, we will box that playgue in. My guys can stop that playgue with our *magician check down coverage.* We will set a boundary on your playgues and *turn them back inside.*[26]
Moses:	Okay but beware we have plagues that include air raids and fly sweeps. We will work from a protected pocket with blitz-stunt containment. You will see lots of keepers and scrambles. Our playgues will leave you in the dark.
Pharaoh:	Don't you worry. We will counter with an aggressive Passover defense that includes a stand up nose guard who drops into coverage and a box in defense.
Narrator:	**The kick off occurs. The ball turns into a *Raven* and flies[27] through the end zone. The Ragtags try a dive play into the Nile from a**

pro set **formation** [28] **on first down. Some blood appears on the water, but Royals counter with their own blood pumped from a bloodmobile chariot along the river.** (A drop of wine is spilled from the wine cup.)

The Royals succeed in driving the Ragtag blood back.[29] **Ragtags try an option and end run on second and third downs. Both end up in the river. Once again blood spreads in the Nile but the Royals manage to stop the flow with their defensive tactics. Israelites are forced to kick. The ball goes high and an *arm reaches out from Heaven*[30] holding it until the Egyptian receiver is forced to make a fair catch signal.**

Amun:

The Hyksos referee is signaling that the Israelites first playgue[31] was stopped for no gain.

Moses:

Pharaoh you must let my people go to worship our God or your land will be subject to another terrible playgue. This time frogs will invade every nook and cranny of Egypt. The Nile shall swarm with frogs and you won't be able to contain them.

Pharaoh:

My guys can match that tricky playgue. Our defenders will split the gap[32] and force the frogs to scram. The Israelites won't gain anything again.

Moses:

Yes but your people will suffer. We will leap frog over your defenses. (A drop of wine is spilled from the wine cup)

Act II

Scene 2
Frogs

Narrator:	**The Israelites run three jumping style plays releasing frogs at the end of each but the Royals hold them back by releasing their own frogs. The result is frogs everywhere.**
Pharaoh:	Okay plead with your remote 'I am' to remove the frogs from our land and I will let your people go.
Moses:	Okay. But when do you want this departure to take place?
Pharaoh:	How about tomorrow?
Moses:	Right. The frogs will stay in the water but we will clean them off the land.
Pharaoh:	Oh I changed my mind. I am not sure why. Nobody leaves.[33]
Hyksos:	The second playgue has failed. The Royals now have the ball.
Narrator:	**The Royals run and pass the ball for three downs without any gain.**

Pharaoh (Faro):   It's fourth down. Where are the punters? We need a punter.

Poti-go: We sent in a punter. Yes, we must find the best way to Punt.[34]

Narrator: **The punter kicks the ball. Angels grab it in the air and it floats softly and lovingly toward the Ragtag deep receiver.**

Act II

Scene 3
Gnats

Amun:

Oh my god, it looks like the Israelites have gone to a quick snap play. *No warning* to Pharoah this time. Moses & Aaron are scraping the ground and stirring up a pile of dust and lice.

Bayisru:

Yeah this looks like a flea flicker[35] playgue. The Royal coaches are also beating the dust to defeat it, but for the first time they can't stop it on their own. They are trying all kinds of stunts but they can't get good coverage on it.

Amun:

Thuti is down on the field. She is listening to an exchange between Pharoah and his assistant coaches.

Thuti: Thanks Amun. The assistant coaches told Pharaoh that the lice playgue is 'the finger of God.' Pharaoh asked *which finger* [36] it was, but the assistants decided not to reveal that. Pharaoh became angry. He wouldn't listen to them nor would he let the Israelites have their way.

Hyksos: The third playgue has gained some yardage. The Ragtags stay on offense when we playgue again to begin the second quarter. (A drop of wine is spilled from the wine cup.)

Game Time: Second Quarter Playgues: Wild Beasts; Pestilence; Boils

Act III

Scene 1
Sci-Fi: Insects become Wild Beasts

Narrator: **Pharaoh is emerging from a morning swim in the Nile and is confronted by Moses. Playgues four to six: Wild beasts; Murrain or Pestilence (a cattle affliction); and Boils (a human skin affliction)- are coming up. In the fourth plague, Wild Beasts attack only the Royals and their fans, but not the Israelites. This plague is devastating for the Egyptians. The roar of the crowd turns into moans and groans of some intensity.** (A drop of wine is spilled from the wine cup.)

Moses:
I just got word that our next playgue will be an insect swarming attack. The Insects are so big that they become wild beasts. Your people will suffer infestation in their homes, businesses, and other locations. But you will notice that some sections of the stands and in Egypt will be free of this plague. That will happen where my fans are located.[37] I will give you a day to consider before I signal this playgue into the game.

Pharaoh:
Advisor, what is our defense?

Potti-go:
We are going to use a box eight upfront. That defense along with corner backs and a roaming deep safety will contain these beasts. We should be able to stir up some real crowd noise *against this playgue.*[38]

Pharaoh:
What if I tell Moses and Aaron that they can sacrifice to their God right here in Egypt?

Poti-phar:	Good idea. Our fans are ready to get even for what the Israelite have made them undergo. Let's get them involved. [38]

Pharaoh:	Okay summon Moses and Aaron.

Narrator: **Moses and Aaron Arrive**

Pharaoh:	Okay Moses, I am prepared to make a concession to you Israelites. How about you plan to sacrifice to your God right here in Egypt?

Moses:	No way Ramzay. Your fans will see that that doesn't happen.

Pharaoh:	Okay-how about you go a short distance, maybe a few yards outside of the country. And for that I expect that you will plead with your God that he remove the wild beasts that are besieging us and our people . (A drop of wine is spilled)

Moses:	Okay, I will do that but make sure that you are not being deceitful with us.

Narrator: **Moses and Aaron leave the area.**

Pharaoh:	As soon as the wild beasts are removed by the Israelite God, I will change my mind and not let the Israelites go. As soon as we are on offense, we will run QB keepers and scrambles against their 'box-in-defense.' Something is telling me to do that in spite of some of your advice.

Narrator: **The next day, Moses shows up at Pharaoh's opulent palace.**

Act III

Scene 2
Pestilence

Moses:	Oh Pharaoh. You seem to welcome disaster. Okay to this point we haven't destroyed your property and your people. So our next playgue, pestilence, will decimate your livestock and devastate your people. The livestock of the Israelites will, however, not be diseased just to be sure you and the people know that this is not the result of *natural causes.*[39]
Narrator:	**Pharaoh calls a time out and huddles with his assistant coaches.**
Pharaoh:	Do we have a defense?
Poti-Near:	Let's try zone coverage to keep this playgue under control.
Narrator:	**The Pestilence playgue succeeds. Moses agrees to Pharaoh's promises and God's decision to lift it.**
Pharaoh:	Okay what if they continue to pass?
Potti-go:	Well if it looks like they are taking to the skies and are going airborne. We will go into man to man coverage with the free safety ready to double their prime receiver, Joshua.[40]

Act III

Scene 3
Boils

Moses   From your own kilns, Aaron and I will throw soot into the air and that soot will carry severe infection to the skin of your fans. Your people will be greatly discomfited and break out in boils. (A drop of wine is spilled from the wine cup.)

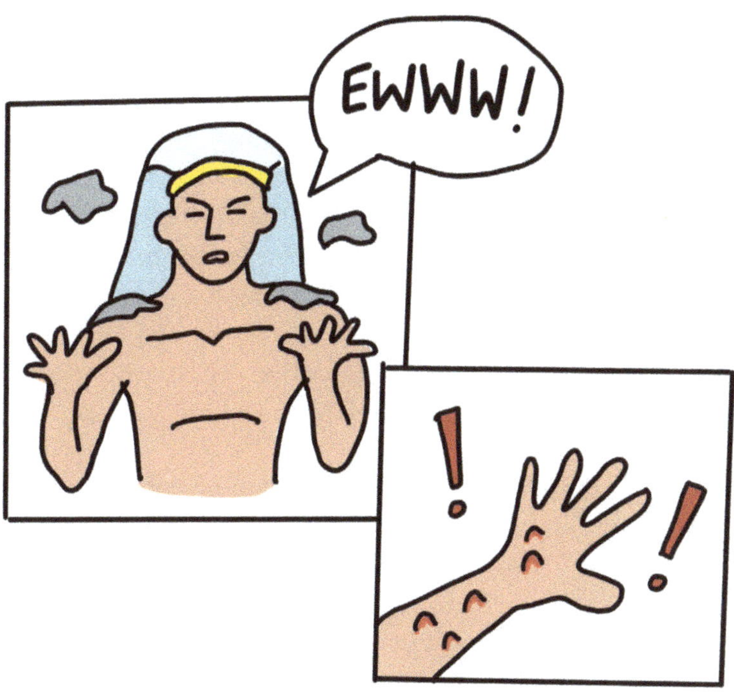

Pharaoh: What defenses shall we use against the sixth boil playgue?

Poti-far: Their Boil playgue will be put into effect with a deep soot fake handoff and a throw into the air. I say we go to double safeties with deep area responsibilities and have the line backers cover their zones. That should keep the soot under control.

Narrator: The playgues work but the Ragtags are still not the winners. Pharaoh and his court return to their Pyramid Locker room bedraggled and seemingly defeated.

Pharaoh: Well they carried out six playgues, but I am not going to yield on their request. I may be too stubborn and I am not sure why that is so, but somehow that's how I feel.

Poti-near:

I get the feeling that they are trying to run up the tally at this point. It looks like they could have finished us off with their prior playgues. But they must want to insure that they make an impression on everyone just in case there is any question left about who proved what to whom. It will also demoralize others who may wish to challenge them. It's a ratings game.

Half Time: Narrated Sponsor Ads

Narrator:

Chariots for sale-new and used –good for warfare; with and without blade attachments; rear entry; fits two people comfortably; not suitable for water crossing.

Camel feed -Great cpm- cubits per meal; all wheat diet cuts down on spitting at people.

Plague insurance-Keep plagues away from your door - not included in regular policies.

Nectar and Ambrosia-Drink divinely but responsibly.

Half Time Shows

Narrator:

A battle of the Bands of Brothers: The Four Sons versus the Four Questions[41] Participants are invited to suggest appropriate song titles and lyrics such as: I can't Give You anything but Love; Ain't Misbehaving; My Immortal; Skydust; You are too good to be true; Hallelujah; The Sun Ain't Gonna Shine; I Just Can't Help Believing; Insects Keep

Falling on My Head; Hey, Won't You Playgue; and Somebody Done Something Wrong; and Who's Sorry Now.

Narrator: The half time score is Royals 0 and the Ragtags 6. But the spread is nine so there's a long way to go. The Half Time ends.

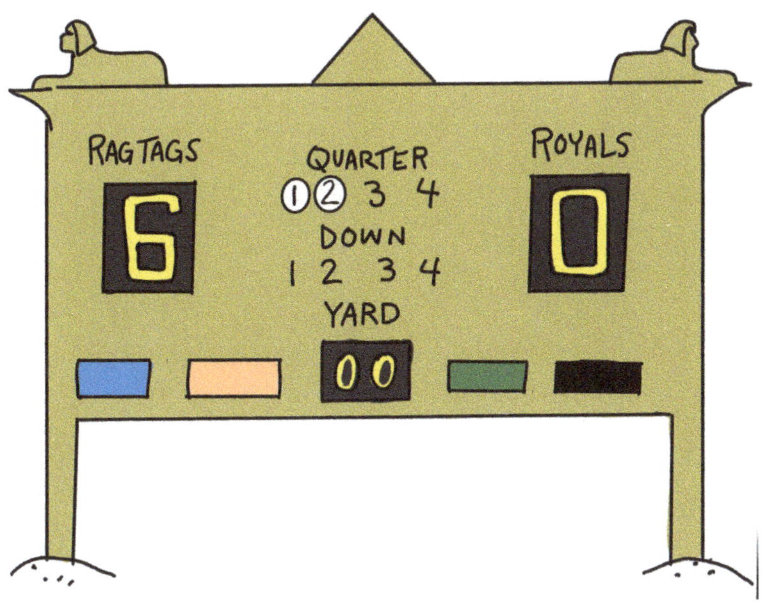

Narrator: Third Quarter **Playgues are: Hail- Locusts- Darkness.**

Act IV

Scene 1
Hail

Moses:	Now you should know that the real intentions of the Lord, the God of the Hebrews. He has, to this point, spared you and your team from being effaced from the earth for the purpose of displaying just how powerful He is to the whole world.
Pharaoh:	What are you talking about?
Moses:	We have shown you how the Lord can effect every aspect of your country. Then God divided the Egyptians from the Israelites to show how much control he had over his game plan. Now in our next playgue He will divide your people between those who respond to my next playgue, which is Hail. Torrents of hail will not destroy any Israelite livestock and property or Egyptian livestock or property, which is brought indoors. This playgue should show you who is still with you and who is against you. Those Egyptians who bring their livestock and property indoors will be indicating that they have lost faith in you.[42]
Pharaoh:	Quickly Poti-advisors- What is our defense?
Poti-near:	There are a lot of options at play here. One is to green dog Wily linebacker. He will blitz[43] if his man stays home. Maybe he will sack their

QB Moses for a big loss and knock the hail out of him. Another is a 3-3-5 defense which will provide an umbrella against the hail.

Potti-go: Good. Use the umbrella defense. It will protect us from a Hail Miriam. The front three should keep their passer in the pocket.

Narrator: **With that, Moses raised his arm to the sky. Heavy Hail, thunder, and lightning occurred devastating man and nature. Whatever was not moved indoors or belonged to the Israelites was destroyed.**

Pharaoh: Many of you Poti-people have stayed loyal to me and have lost much. What is your advice at this time?

Poti-near: We must go into a prevent defense including you taking blame upon yourself and admitting that your game plan hasn't worked. Admit that you were wrong and offer to let them go if the hail and thunder and lightning are stopped.)[43] (Spill a drop of blood from the wine cup.)

Pharaoh: You mean give up?

Potti-go: No as soon as the conditions get better you will change your mind and not let them go? I get the feeling that will at least keep us alive for whatever is in store for us.

Act IV

Scene 2

Locusts

Narrator: **Moses and Aaron appear before Pharaoh at the Nile.**

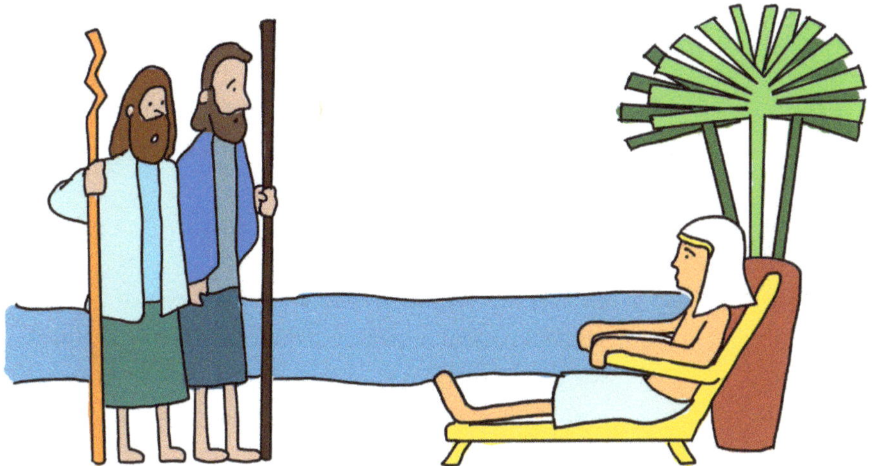

Moses: So Pharaoh, you want to play with a hard nose-guard. We will show you hard! A little bit of wheat remains in the land. As of tomorrow, you can say so long to that food. Locusts using a *spread formation* [44] will descend upon your land and utterly devour any grain or trees still standing. You think you know about the sight of a horde of locusts descending on your land, but this will outdo your wildest imagination or the memory of your entire history, as far as locust swarms are concerned. Tomorrow you will be plagued by a locust swarm like you, your people, and your land have never before experienced. (A drop of wine is spilled from the wine cup.)

Narrator: **Moses turns abruptly and leaves Pharaoh without direction or permission. He turns his back on Pharaoh.**

The next day Pharaoh meets with his assistant] coaches.

Poti-near: I can't see the field of play. It has become dark because of the swarms of locusts.[45]

Potti-go: All the trees and all the fruit have been devoured. There is nothing green to be seen.

Pharaoh: So team what are we going to do?

Poti-near: Coach and god, I think we have had it. They seem to have ways of conducting playgues that we can't stop. And I understand that they have just started the main part of their Passover game.

Narrator: **Moses and Aaron enter and appear before Pharaoh**

Moses:	You must humble yourself before God.
Pharaoh:	Okay supposing I release you. Who do you intend to take with you?
Moses:	All of our team, our fans, our young and old, our flocks and our herds.
Pharaoh:	What! I never thought you were asking for so many to go. No to that group, although you can take your men and go.
Moses:	So much for your *free release ploy.*[47]

Pharaoh: I am guilty of guile and illegal offenses. Forgive me and ask the Lord your God to remove this scourge from my land. (A drop of wine is spilled from the wine cup.)

Narrator: **Moses acts and a wind arises and blows the locusts away.**

Act IV

Scene 3
Darkness

Hyksos: All the Ragtag playgues since the Leaping Frogs have made first downs but no scores. The Ragtags do seem to be headed for the Reed Zone and have been in possession for most of the contest. They still have the control of the playgues.

Pharaoh: I think that we outlasted their God. What more could He do? I changed my mind. The Israelites will not be allowed to go!

God's voice off stage: Moses. Moses. Hold out you hand toward the sky that there may be a severe darkness on the land.[48]

Moses: What no warning this time? Not even a huddle?[49]

God:

No this is an audible. I have noticed that they have been watching for signs and symbols from you and Aaron. They are starting to violate the neutral zone in order to intercept our playgues. I will cut off their full field of vision using a smoke route. This is a *run play with a passing option* [50]depending on what defensive alignment they decide on. Our pattern and the ball will be hidden and we will end up right near the goal line.

Moses:

What about my team?

God:

Do not worry. You will have *light* [51]in your dwellings. After all that's what started my whole project years ago. This playgue directly confronts the so called Sun god and runs right over him.

Moses:

I am not sure what you mean.

God:

I mean that we are going to run right over Pharaoh's strength which is that he is supposed to be the sun god. We have to keep our eyes open while the Royals lose their way in the darkness.[52] (A drop of wine is spilled from the wine cup)

Narrator:

Moses holds up his arm toward the sky. Thick darkness envelopes the land.

Pharaoh:

Now it is our turn to use nature on them. We deserve better field conditions. At least, the skies will be sunny again. That's my strength.I will *call upon the sun* to pierce the darkness.[53]

Narrator:

A mad scramble arises. Egyptian magicians, fans, and cheerleaders run hither and yon

	trying to support Pharaoh's attempt to cause the sun to shine. All to no avail.
Hyksos:	Big gain for the Ragtags. They are at pay dirt and still have playgue control.
Pharaoh:	What shall we do now?
Potti-go:	Maybe we will be fortunate and they will call the contest on account of darkness?
Hyksos:	No there is light where there should be light. The contest will continue and it is time to begin the fourth quarter.

Act V

Scene 1

Prelude to Death of the Egyptian First born

Narrator:	**As the fourth quarter begins, Pharaoh again meets with Moses and Aaron on the Field. Torches provide light. During the fourth and final quarter, Playgue 10- Death of the First Born- will descend upon the Egyptians.**
Pharaoh:	You may go but you have to leave your flocks and herds behind.
Moses:	Not only will we go with our entire flocks and our herds, but you will have to come up with the

animals for our burnt offerings and sacrifices that we plan to make to our God. [54] In that way, your defeat will be complete.

Pharaoh:

No way. The only thing that is going to go at this time is you from my sight. And don't let me see you again because, rules of the game be damned, you are definitely going to be on the 'did not play because of injury' list if you ever do show up in my territory again.

Moses:

You can bet on that, Pharaoh. That threat is going on our locker room scroll. Wait til you see our next playgue. It one for the ages.

Narrator:

God speaks to Moses who is still in front of Pharaoh, but only Moses can interact with or hear God.

God's Voice:

Moses. Moses. Here is the last and most significant playgue. It will be talked about at home and abroad for generations to come. It is a game changer

Moses:

What is going to happen?

God:

After this playgue, Pharaoh will not only let you go, he will force you to leave one and all.

Moses:

What's my role?

God:

Tell our people that they must be prepared for an *18 1/2 minute warning.*[55] Before that they must seek to obtain from their neighbors objects of silver and gold as well as weapons and their playbooks. Don't worry, after what they have been through with our playgues, the neighbors will not be so sad that we are leaving. I do note however that you have *gained respect among the leaders and people of Egypt.*[56] Congratulations.

Moses: Everybody loves a winning playoff team. Is that it as far as my role in this final plague goes?

God: Once I stop playing with Pharaoh's mind, he may make some other bad calls. So see to it that we also have as many weapons and gold-silver items as we can obtain as we leave

Moses: Anything else? What will this playgue accomplish?

God: It will strike **"… down every Egyptian first born and (execute) judgment on their gods."**[57] (A drop of wine is spilled from the wine cup,)

Narrator: **God talks to Moses but it is not heard by others. Moses turns to Pharaoh**

Moses: Toward midnight 'I am that I am's' messenger will go forth among all the Egyptians. From Pharaoh to the slave girl at the millstone all the first born among them shall die, including cattle. Then you will send your Poti-heads to me. They will bow low and say that I and all my people with all our belongings shall depart.

Narrator: **Moses angrily turns from Pharaoh. But Pharaoh shakes his head-No. The scene shifts back to the field area. Moses and Aaron appear before the Israelites who are still in the bleachers. The Israelite cheerleaders wave papyrus leaves and lead the fans in a chant; Moses Moses he's our man; if he can't do it**

nobody can. One fan yells out,"We love you Moses." Another fan yells,"You too Aaron."

Moses: We are down to the final playgue. Everything is riding on it. It illustrates that old saying.'what goes around comes around.' [58] But do not view this as an ending. Rather God has in mind that this is really the beginning. We may have a dynasty here.

Narrator: **In spite of the many displays of God's might, murmurs of unhappiness kept being directed at Moses and Aaron. Finally, the leaders firmly but sympathetically spoke to the Israelites.**

Moses: You have heard the Egyptian cheers and our groans. Now you will hear their groans louder than ever. But their anger will be directed away from us and you must acquire as many objects of silver and gold as well as weapons from your neighbors as you can. We are planning to mold such objects into sanctuary structures in which we will store our own valuable possessions.[59]

Aaron: Just to let you know that we are so sure of victory after this next playgue that we will plan our victory celebration now. We will have a festive meal but then we have to leave quickly to get on our way for this is not our home field and one can never be sure of what can happen. Stay inside until the signal to leave is given. You will be protected. our opponents will not be.

Moses: This *form of celebration* [60]will go through many changes in future years, but the essence of our victory here under the leadership of God and the performance of our Ragtag team will always form its foundation.

Act V

Scene 2

Death of the First Born Egyptian Son

Narrator:	**Back in the Playgue by Playgue Announcers' Booth.**

Amun:

The Ragtags are now setting up their final playgue. It looks like it will be a pass over the heads of the Royals. The Ragtags are in a spread wing formation with three wide outs ready to wreak havoc down field.

Bayirsu:

Yes it looks like they will do their destruction quickly and then just keep on running out of the territory with all deliberate speed. All of their fans will join them in a mass exodus as soon as Pharaoh concedes defeat. Wait- there's Pharaoh now. Thuti are you on top of what's happening?

Thuti:

Yes, I am down on the field and am witnessing the devastation of the Royals entire team and supporters. The Royal fans are starting to desert the team. The Ragtags are doing a lot of high fives. Here is Pharoah who wants to say few words.

Pharaoh:

That final Passover playgue really got to us. Okay, you Israelites can go worship your God for *three days*.[61] You take everyone and also your cattle for the sacrifice that you talked about. But before you go, be good sports and say something nice about us to your God as you sacrifice to him. In any case get him to stop this last playgue which really hurt the families of our side. Our people fear that they will all be dead if this playgue continues.

Moses:	Announcement to the Israelites and others. That's it. Move out with whatever you can carry and whatever you can make to eat in about 18 and 1/2 minutes. Our Exodus will be our victory parade. God will be with us and stand guard over our departure. Never forget this day and the Passover and the playgues that led to our freedom. Observe this victory where ever you may end up but particularly in the land of milk and honey that I have promised you.The Royals tried to destroy our sons; we destroyed their sons; and now our first sons belong to God who led us to victory Playgue after Playgue. What a game plan!

Act V

Scene 3

Post Game Interviews

Narrator: **We now have a hasty post game Q & A with the Press. On stage are Aaron, Moses, and Miriam. The Moderator is Pliny the Elder.**

Pliny: Who has the first question? Yes, the scribe in the back.

Reporter # 1: Senebkay of the Lower Nile News: Aaron, how do you feel about how things playgued out?

Aaron: Pharaoh was stubborn. A formidable foe. But the accuracy of our playgues and our offensive time on the field overcame what the Royals could do playing defense. God's hand offs and passes displayed a mighty hand and arm which would not be denied. We will face many challenges in the future, but this event is an historic encounter. We beat them offensively, defensively, and with our special team effects. These records will be preserved forever.

Pliny: Next question?

Reporter #2: Woseribe of the *Abydos Sentinel*; Moses, what do you think was the turning point in this contest?

Moses: Well we stuck to our game plan and we kept ratcheting up the pressure. At first, we worked on general things that the Royals understood and in fact could match. Our ability to get to their leader for sacks and knockdowns turned the tide. Then we moved to areas that showed that we could pick our spots and attack them without hurting ourselves. We switched our offense from natural destructive playgues to option playgues to a Passover playgue which was way beyond their ability to adjust. Those playgues as well as the others were sent in to us, we claim no credit for them.

Pliny: Next question?

Reporter #3: Beitzel of the *Goshen Gazette*: What about your fans-how did they react to the playgues?

Aaron: Well to tell the truth, we were a little dismayed by the reaction of our fans. In the beginning, there was a lot of griping about this or that hardship that resulted from the Royals' defensive efforts including more work with less resources. But as time went by and different playgues moved us toward the Red Sea zone, the complaints were much less. The final playgue offered a way of getting out of Egypt. It worked well and everyone cooperated.

Pliny: Last question.

Reporter #4: Mandlin of the *Middle Kingdom Trib*: Miriam, How do you feel about how things developed?

Miriam: I remember Moses when he was just a kid in a cradle. Now he's a celebrity. And How about that Aaron? He certainly is a star in his own right. I am so proud of my brothers and, of course, of the one who is 'I am that I am.' Our captains and coach had an awesome game plan. We used the initial plagues to soften opposing defense alignments and counter actions, Then I Am went right after the idea that Pharaoh is a sort of an unbeatable Sun god. The darkness playgue revealed the weakness of that claim. The sun did not shine at all. And then I Am followed with the Passover strategy for which Pharaoh had no defense at all. It was game over!

Pliny: Okay that wraps things up now. Our three presenters have to get away now. They have heard that they will have to change routes on their way out.

Moses, Aaron, and Miriam make a quick exit. They explain that they have an appointment with 'I Am' at Mt. Sinai.

Act V

Scene 4
Final Narration

Narrator:	**Thus it was that the final playgue in the contest enabled the formation of an ethical monotheistic belief system, which would be recognized throughout the world. There would be a continuation of the contest in overtime as they made their way home. That battle too, however, would result in another victory for the Ragtag Israelties with a defiant defense in the Sea of Reeds zone. Appendix III titled *Sudden Death Overtime*-provides a script for that scene if desired.**

The result of the plagues, the overtime, and the 40 year journey with all of its historic significance through the wilderness brought the Israelites to the land promised by God. They were then armed with a miraculous rebirth experience and a theological code of human conduct and responsibility. A dynasty was born that through many tough future events has lasted to this moment. (Sing *Dayenu* and *Go Down Moses.)*

The Passover plate symbols (Pashal lamb; Matzah, and bitter herbs) are now presented and explained. Hallel is recited. A second cup of wine is blessed and drunk. Wash hands. Bless the matzah remaining in the matzah plate on the table. Dip bitter herbs into

charoses, say the blessing and eat the bitter and the sweet on the matzah (Korech.) The children find the Afikomen. The meal is eaten and the remainder of the Seder may follow a conventional Haggadah in its order and ritual.

EXODUS PLAN

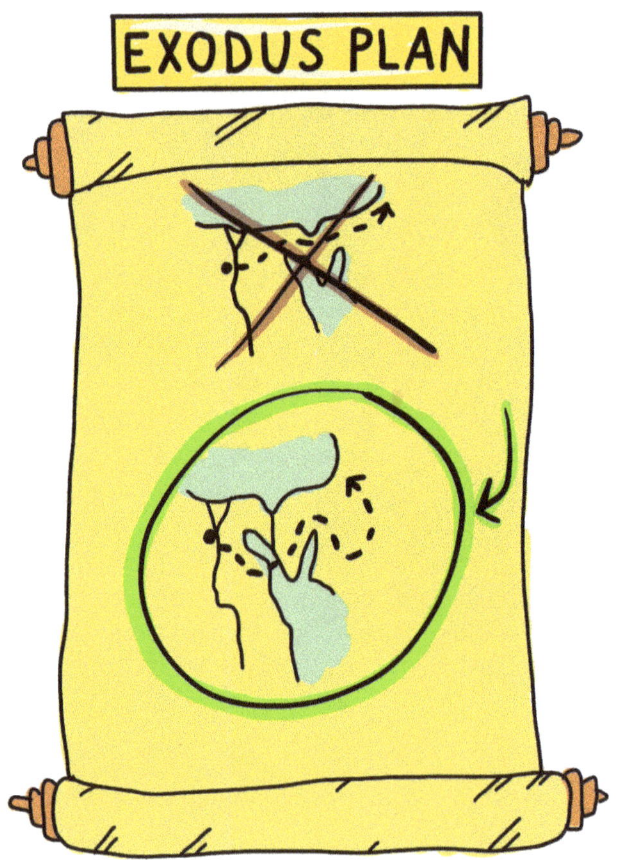

Numbered Footnotes

1   Ragtags conveys not only material poverty but spiritual hopelessness. Somehow the Israelite community hung together. Perhaps it was enslavement itself that enabled them to remain a Kahila (bonded community.)

2   The final 10th plague Death of the First Born makes the Israelites victorious.

3   Numbers of Jacob's family said to have arrived in Egypt initially. Foretold to Abram by God in Gen.15:13.The growth in numbers of Israelites to a huge population is anticipated in Gen 46:8-27

4   Include for readings. For more elaborate productions, have people make signs, pictures, etc. and present them in creative ways.

5   Discuss differences between such different worship forms.

6   The world stage

7   A much more regional focus

8   Pharaoh proposes a number of less than desirable 'escape' plans to the Israelites. NFL coaches use option plays to confuse opponents and to take advantage of them.

9   Good chance to review Moses birth, background, and relation to family. His father was Amram and his mother, Jochebed. Moses had an older brother Aaron and an older sister, Miriam. The family was of the tribe of Levi.

10   Moses was a Prince of Egypt and then an exile. Review how that happened.

11   A Pharaoh 'who knew not Joseph.' Review some of the meanings of that phrase. The death of the king who ordered Moses into exile (Exodus 1:23), paved the way for his return to Egypt to appear before the new Pharaoh.

12   Try to get guest, participants, and audience to elaborate, add to, and pun any of these suggestions. Temper them to the attendees if some are too adult

13   No huddle just God instructing Moses and Aaron as the playgues unfold one by one. Formation enables Moses to see the whole field and keep Pharaoh on the defense. Shotgun formation often used for quick snaps. Ask what defense should be used if more emphasis on football tactics is desired by those in attendance

14   What reasons can you think of for Pharaoh to be stubborn? And why does God harden Pharaoh's heart.

15   A spoof on the coin toss sequence.

16   The plagues are announced to Pharaoh at these two locations.

17   Caleb is the first scout (#11) who urges Moses and the Israelites to go ahead with God's initial plan to enter and take over the promised land. Joshua agrees with Caleb, but ten other scouts urge caution.

18   Exodus III:14 Some scholars believe that the Israelites originated from this group or enjoyed their favor while they ruled Egypt for over 100 years.

19   Exodus III

20   Exodus VI: 14 A relationship that transcends time, space, and current conditions. This reminder has philosophical, spiritual, and ethnic overtones [23]

21   Exodus VII:8-11 A spoof of the coin toss before football games.

22   Exodus VII: 12

23   RA was considered the chief and most powerful god among many of Egypt. PhaRAoh associated himself closely with this Sun god by name and by custom

24   Hillbilly cutoff shorts and form fitting tops made household words by Jewish cartoonist Al Capp in the mid-20th century.

25   Further background going back to Joseph's dreams, journey, and experience in Canaan and Egypt. Balak; Daniel; Job) depending on factors and circumstances

26   Outside men have to prevent running backs from getting outside the defensive ends and linebackers.In this context, it means that Pharoah is determined to keep the Israelites as slaves.

27   Just a touch of Game of Thrones

28   If appropriate to age group and football knowledge of participants ask questions about this offense:-strengths, used when, variations, etc. Also ask what defense works best against it.

29   The Egyptian magicians were able to stop the blood from spreading and duplicated the Israelites ability to create blood in the Nile.

30   More special effect for fun. Prevents a Royals run back.

31   Hashem is testing the water of the Royals sacred river and setting up for the next Playgue : Frogs.

32   Football talk indicating finding holes in the offensive line and disrupting the play

33 God is manipulating Pharaoh's mind In order to be sure that this story becomes well known in the entire region. The power of God in defeating Egypt must be recognized as formidable at this time and in these circumstances as not just a fluke or an upset quick victory of some sort.

34 Punt was a major trading center in the mid-East at the time of the Pharaohs. Due to desert sand storms and other natural conditions, the ' best way to Punt' often had to be redetermined. Finding the safest, shortest, and best route to it was a constant and shifting struggle for the nations of the area. Since trade was so important, finding the best way to Punt was important.

35 This is the third plague. It came with no warning from Moses as playgues one and two did. Situation is intensifying. In this trick play the QB hands off to a running back who then turns and flips the ball back to the QB. The QB then throws a pass.

36 An adult joke. May not be appropriate for children

37 Important distinction. Starts to inflict pain on Egyptians, but exempts Israelites from it. Likely to cause pressure to resolve the issue by the Egyptian people directed at Pharaoh and his Priests.

38 Effort to direct anger toward Israelites and their God and away from Pharaoh. If Egyptians suffer but Israelites don't, they, it is hoped, will turn against the Israelites. Turn the crowd around.

39 Many researchers have suggested that these playgues are just nature taking its course. Blood in the Nile forces the frogs onto land where they die and their carcasses bring gnats and other insects and so on. This differentiation highlights why that explanation does not hold and the universal impact of the divine element of the story is intensified.

40 Looking ahead, Joshua will receive the leadership role when Moses dies at 120. Moses is 80 now.

41 Review these readings, Ask which segment adds most to the educational, cultural, and intergenerational experience at the Seder

42 Here the strategy continues to unfold. Even Pharaohs have limitations as to how far they can expect their subjects to stay loyal in the face of great difficulties. Now God advises Egyptians that they can preserve their property by taking care of it.in a prescribed way. The Egyptians will now begin to ask themselves what is in their best interest and add to the pressure of Pharaoh's advisors to let the Israelites go

43 Use the weak side linebacker to rush the QB and throw him for a loss or worse.

44 One of the most productive offensive formations. Since locust storms were not unknown in Egypt, Moses goes to great pains to differentiate the devastation with which the Egyptians will now be faced with. Their ancestors, and all of Egypt have never seen nor heard of. The locusts will scavenge your crops, fill your palaces, make your homes unlivable, and your lives unbearable (Spill a drop of blood from the wine cup)

45 Exodus 10:3-6 Locust swarms did occur in Egypt from time to time. But this swarm promised to be the most devastating ever.

46 Exodus 9:27-35 In an effort to undermine Moses, Pharaoh admits the guilt of himself and his people. By this action, he hopes to trick Moses into accepting his terms for letting the Israelites go.

47 Moses realizes that only if the whole cohort of Israelites go free will it be clear that monotheism, and an unseen all powerful, merciful, moral God exists as the only true divinity. Pharaoh and his advisers and dazzled by the coordination of the many tactics involved. The 'call' recognizes that the Royals are getting desperate.

48   Complete and total darkness is frightening.

49   God is now challenging directly the power of the SUN god the principal god of Egypt and the one that Pharaoh aligns himself with. God is now directly involved.

50   This plague raises the bar on a display of the strength of God. We are in the final stages of insuring that the Royals are completely demoralized

51   Genesis 1:3. On the first day, God said let there be light. Metaphorically that is the light that leads men to morality through the spirit of God..

52   xodus 10:21 … darkness that can be touched. Anyone who has encountered desert darkness can appreciate how devastating this pitched black is. It is indeed just one step below and a prelude to the darkness of death.

53   Pharaoh decides to throw his whole status into the contest. If his sun penetrates the darkness he can overcome the Israelites and their God.

54   The final twist. This act will signify the capitulation of Pharaoh to God although Pharaoh will try one more attempt to snatch victory from defeat.

55   This is a play on the NFL 2 minute warning at half time and before the end of the game as well as the suggested time that the Israelites had to prepare Matzoh for their use on the road.

56   Another problem for Pharaoh

57   Numbers 33.4

58   As Pharaoh initially decreed the death of all new male children now God's act reminds him of that terrible decision and trumps

it with by decreeing the death of all of the Egyptian first born including the Pharaoh's son.

59   Anticipation and planning for the Ark of the Covenant.

60   The family centered Passover Seder

61   Exactly what the Israelites demanded at first

62   Some commentators suggest that this direction at the water's edge represents a decision by God to stop being totally in charge. Moses is now a leader of a nation and must start making decisions for it. Just as a Quarterback is a leader of a team and must decide on the spot what to do. A new human to divine trust and relationship is being established and will soon be manifest on Mt.Sinai..

Appendices

A. Other Titles of Sports Interest

B. Production and Performamce Tips

C. Post Game: Sudden Death Overtime in the Reeds Zone

D. List of Ten Related Study Questions

E. Animals in the Hebrew Bible: Possible Mascots

F. Defeated Egyptian gods and goddesses

Appendix I
Other Titles Of Sports Interest

Titles from the *Jewish Ancient History and Modern Sports* series are listed below. Please support these performances in theaters, on TV, and in group therapy.

Baseball means Diamonds: Stop Running in Circles-make a few bucks.

Basketball under the Chupa: Crash the Glass.

Crossfit Circumcision: Work the Angles.

Fencing Phalacteries: Don't get strapped in.

Football Fantasy: Pigskin or Foreskin.

Field Hockey and Havdalah: Elijah is the Insert.

Golf is for Goyem: Don't Drive on Shabbat or Festivals.

Ice Hockey in Israel: Just to say we can.

LaCrosse is Us: Moses was born with a cradle & Aaron was a great stick handler.

Polo on the Green: Okay but you still have to pull the plow.

Soccer in the Sukkah: Put your head into the Schach.

Softball Sense: Proverbs - She who leaves the base early will be rebuked and called out.

Swimming for Swarma: Wipe your face boychik

Water Polo in the Promised Land: Is the Mikveh big enough?

Wrestling with Angels: Why be Jewish?

Volleyball Voices: Sett(l)ers and Strikers.

Yoga during Yom Kippur: Fast but not Furious.

Appendix II
Production and Performance

This little playlet may be overly ambitious. Efforts should be made to make it informative, entertaining, and educational including cutting out sections, shortening monologues, and speeding up cues. In some cases, these omissions may require a line or two adjustment to insure that a proper transition takes place and confusion about what is being presented is cleared up.

I. Below we have suggested some segments that may be omitted. Eliminating them all would probably not be good practice because originally everything had its purpose individually and narratively. Yet, some actions may be warranted given performance conditions. Please think it through though because your decisions may injure the whole purpose of the playlet. Leader judgment re: omissions is encouraged. These ideas are meant as possibilities only.

II. Segments that may be considered for Omission:

   A. On page 4 and part of page 5: Pregame Broadcast Booth Scene

B. Motivational Raps and next two lines by Amun and Bayisru on page 6.
C. Lines on Page 7 up to Game Time First Quarter
D. All narration in first, second, third, and fourth Quarters. Only dialogue remains.
E. Halftime Ads, Shows, selected narration, and dialogue.
F. Post game Interviews
G. On the Exodus Road.
H. Sudden Death Overtime
I. Comments and discussion can be limited or extensive.

Appendix III

Overtime

The other side of this coin is to expand on the matters raised in this playlet. Perhaps it could be used over a period of time to prepare students and others for a fuller appreciation of all that is involved for Jews in making the Seder an uplifting, educational, and cultural experience. Maybe it can be the basis for a second or third seder or a Sunday School presentation before the Seders take place.

Our commentary is merely suggestive. Teachers and knowledgeable lay people can examine many more items raised by the narrative in real depth and in a more extensive horizon of Jewish and non-Jewish history.

Please however be cautious not to fall into the trap of sermonizing or being didactic. The American Football motif is more than an excuse to entice children and others to learn about Jewish history and practices. Rather it is an invitation to them to realize how vibrant and 'right now' their heritage can be and how creative they should be in making it relevant to their lives. If they stop reading, listening, and laughing, change the style and the script!

Cast for the Postgame and Overtime Scenes

Moses; Aaron; Poti-far; Pharaoh; Poti-near; Popti-go; Nachshon

Scene 1 The Ragtags are on the road. Moses is arguing as if talking on a blue tooth.

Moses: You got to be kidding. You want us to go the long way. How are Aaron and I going to explain that instruction? Okay so, there are forts along the northern route and you still think these guys aren't ready to really defend themselves even though they do have weapons that the Egyptians provided as we pulled up stakes in their country by night. And you've made note of the fact that our people may have to shake the chains of slavery from their beings as well as their status.

Aaron: Did I hear that right? We are going the long way! It looks like we are headed into a water trap.

Moses: God will guide us-watch for a pillar of cloud by day and a pillar of fire by night.

Aaron: My guess is that God is still not satisfied that our people, the Egyptians, and the world are convinced about His power and authority. Something is afoot here besides this mixed multitude behind us.

Moses: Well we have been on the road for three days and now we have to get across this water. I asked coach about our situation.

Aaron: What did he say?

Moses: He said 'Don't ask me. Call something.'[62]

Scene 2 Post Game: Sudden Death Over Time

Meanwhile back at the Palace, Pharaoh is meeting with his advisers.

Poti-far: You shouldn't have let them go.

Pharaoh: Sure you say that now- you Moonday morning quarterback. Where were you when all the moaning and groaning injuries were taking place?

Poti-near: It is not too late. Our scouts tell us that the Israelites are hemmed in in the Red Sea Zone. They have gone astray and seem lost in the wilderness. They have lost their defiance. Let's go get em!

Pharaoh: Yeah, I told them they could only go for three days and that time is up. They should be back here. We need their service.

Poti-go: Get the special teams ready. Two man chariots plan. We haven't lost this one yet.

The scene shifts back to Moses and Aaron and the Israelites with their backs to the Sea.

Aaron: Moses, scouting reports indicate that Pharaoh has his special team of charioteers lined up to come after us. And the people are murmuring. They are talking about going back! They say it is better than losing the contest here.

Moses: Oh my. It looks like we will have to get this march going again to preserve our freedom. I will need some help.

Suddenly, an Israelite, Nachshon, appears and humbly approaches Moses and Aaron. He realizes that the Israelites are in a tough spot.

Nachshon: Moses I am going to jump in to get this mixed multitude going. You have been a messenger of God and have shown us the way to freedom. Now we must all do our part.

Moses: You have my respect and gratitude. Please make your move.

So Nachshon jumped in, Moses held his rod over the sea, the sea split, and the columns of Israelites moved through the sea. The Egyptian chariots followed. They got stuck in the muck, and were engulfed when the wind holding the waters aside lost its forward progress.

Appendix IV
Related Study Questions

Note: In the following choice questions, there are no wrong answers. It is hoped that each of the possibilities will be discussed in terms of Jewish history, scholarship, significance, and ritual at an appropriate level among the assembled.

1. If this contest was a bowl game, which name would you attach to it and why?

    A. Straw Bowl
    B. Supreme Bowl
    C. Slave Bowl
    D. Symbol Bowl.
    E. Seder Bowl

2. Why is there a scene which depicts a person in a multi colored coat wandering around in a field of lean and fat corn and lean and fat cows?

A. Agriculture was the principal industry when the Israelites went to Egypt.
B. Dreams were said to provide important insights into the future.
C. The person wandering was very important to the Exodus story.
D. Dreams are very important explicitly and implicitly to the Exodus story.

3. Consider the scene in which God recruited Moses at the Burning Bush?

A. Why is Moses a first round pick?
B. What was Moses' reaction when God introduced himself?
C. What contract terms were agreed to by Moses and God?
D. What reasons did Moses give for not signing on with the Israelites?
E. How does God persuade Moses to sign the contract?

4. God feels He has been dissed by the Egyptians. He will vindicate his name by:

A. Reintroducing Himself by another name.
B. Reminding Moses of His covenant with Abraham, Isaac, and Jacob.
C. Promising the Israelites liberation and bringing them to a land of their own.
D. The signs and marvels He will bring to bear on his foes in this contest

5. The Game Plan includes.

A. The strategy of the Israelites.
B. The reactions and adjustments of Pharaoh during the contest
C. Many blood references.
D. Many first born son references
E. Aaron playing a significant role as a co-captain and spokesperson.

6. Why did God harden Pharaoh's heart throughout the contest?

   A. God needed a quality win.
   B. Other rivals were scouting the contest and it was important that they think that the Israelites were powerful.
   C. It was good for Israelite's morale and spirit.
   D. The plagues built up the stature of Moses in the eyes of the Israelites.

7. The Egyptian Royals versus the Israelite Ragtags contest is divided into four quarters in accordance with the rules of football. The author decided on a 3-3-3-1 formation by assigning the first three plagues to the first quarter; plagues 4-6 to the second quarter; plagues 7-9 to the third quarter; and the final plague to the fourth quarter. Given the many factors associated (warning/no warning; matched/unmatched ; natural/cultural; etc.) with the plagues, which of the formations do you think make the best sense?

   A. The plagues fit nicely into the 3-3-3-1 format.
   B. The format 2-3-4-1 would be best.
   C. The format 2-4-2-2 would be best.
   D. The format 5-2-2-1 would be best.
   E. No way to convincingly characterize the plagues by groups.

8. The first meeting of Moses and Aaron with Pharaoh resulted in:

   A. Moses and Aaron asking for a delay of game so the Israelites could celebrate a festival for their God away from the bad conditions of Egypt's home field.
   B. Pharaoh stating his reasons for refusing the challenge.
   C. Pharaoh objecting and making the Israelites do grueling two a day practice sessions in the heat.
   D. The Israelite's locker room being filled with dissension.
   E. Ragtag fans taking their complaints directly to Pharaoh.

9. How did the Egyptian people feel about the Israelites as the Playgues unfolded?

   A. Why can't we all get along?
   B. Gods- schmods, we are all slaves really.
   C. Hey, the Israelites might be right.
   D. Go already and take a few of us with you.
   E. Here, take precious metal, some tools, and some weapons with you.

10. Pharaoh has post-game regret and decides to chase the Israelites because:

   A. Pharaoh realizes the implications of his defeat and is looking for redemption.
   B. The Israelites were in a precarious situation hemmed on a shore.
   C. The assistant coaches huddled & urged Pharaoh to run the chariot.play.
   D. God had one more trick He wanted to use.
   E. The three day agreement had run its course.

Appendix V

Animals of the Bible: Possible Mascots

Ass	Goat	Ox
Bat	Hare	Pelican
Badger	Hawk	Ram
Bull	Heron	Scorpion
Camel	Horse	Snake
Cow	Lion	Sheep
Crocodile	Lizard	Stork
Falcon	Mule	Vulture

Frog   Mouse
Gecko   Ostrich
Donkey   Owl

Defeated Egyptian gods and goddesses (the Heliopolis nine and Pharaoh)

Plague	Defeated Egyptian Deity	Title	Placement
Blood	Hapi	Nile Principal god	0-10 yard line
Frogs	Heket	Nile Fertility goddess	10-20 yard line
Gnats	Geb	Earth god	20-30 yard line
Wild Beasts	Khepri	Creation god	30-40 yard line
Pestilence	Hathor	Fertility goddess	40-50 yard line
Boils	Isis	Healing Moon goddess	50-40 yard line
Hail	Nut	Sky goddess	40-30 yard line
Locusts	Set	Desert Storm god	30-20 yard line
Darkness	Ra	The Sun god	20-10 Yard line
Death of First Born	Pharaoh	Living Sun god	10-TD End Zone